Authors • Jessica Blomstrom, Adam Daigle,
Shaun Hocking, Daniel Marthaler, Tork Shaw,
and Christina Stiles

Cover Artist • Michal Ivan

Interior Artists • Marius Bota, Jorge Fares, Diana Martinez,
Emiliano Petrozzi, Bryan Sola, and Xia Taptara

Creative Director • James Jacobs
Editor-in-Chief • F. Wesley Schneider
Senior Editor • James L. Sutter
Development Lead • Adam Daigle
Development Team • Adam Daigle, Rob McCreary,
Mark Moreland, and Patrick Renie
Editorial Team • Judy Bauer, Logan Bonner,
Christopher Carey, and Ryan Macklin
Lead Designer • Jason Bulmahn
Design Team • Stephen Radney-MacFarland and
Sean K Reynolds

Senior Art Director • Sarah E. Robinson
Graphic Designers • Sonja Morris and Andrew Vallas
Production Specialist • Crystal Frasier

Publisher • Erik Mona
Paizo CEO • Lisa Stevens
Chief Operations Officer • Jeffrey Alvarez
Director of Sales • Pierce Watters
Marketing Director • Jenny Bendel
Finance Manager • Christopher Self
Staff Accountant • Kunji Sedo
Chief Technical Officer • Vic Wertz
Senior Software Developer • Gary Teter
Campaign Coordinator • Mike Brock
Project Manager • Jessica Price

Customer Service Team • Cosmo Eisele, Erik Keith,
and Sara Marie Teter
Warehouse Team • Will Chase, Michael Kenway,
Matt Renton, Jeff Strand, and Kevin Underwood
Website Team • Ross Byers, Liz Courts, Lissa Guillet,
and Chris Lambertz

ON THE COVER

Michal Ivan paints a picture of power
and righteousness, showing the iconic
paladin Seelah cutting through a horde
of monsters up to no good.

TABLE OF CONTENTS

REFERENCE

This Pathfinder Player Companion refers to several other Pathfinder Roleplaying Game
products and uses the following abbreviations. These books are not required to make use
of this Player Companion. Readers interested in references to Pathfinder RPG hardcovers can
find the complete rules from these books available for free at **paizo.com/prd**.

Advanced Player's Guide	APG	*Inner Sea Magic*	ISM
Advanced Race Guide	ARG	*Ultimate Combat*	UC
Bestiary 2	B2	*Ultimate Equipment*	UE
Bestiary 3	B3	*Ultimate Magic*	UM

Paizo Publishing, LLC
7120 185th Ave NE, Ste 120
Redmond, WA 98052-0577

paizo.com

D0556602

For Your Character

In every Pathfinder Player Companion, you'll find something for your character. This companion includes the following.

FOCUS CHARACTERS

This Player Companion highlights options specific to characters of the following classes, in addition to elements that can apply to other characters as well.

CLERICS

Often the voice of purity and goodness, clerics lead their flocks and tend to their adventuring parties with wisdom. The new subdomains (page 20) and spells (page 28) in this book add versatility to clerics who follow good deities.

FIGHTERS

Fighting for a living doesn't make you a bad person. Many fighters defend their homeland or fight to help out the less fortunate. A number of magical weapons (page 30), feats (page 23), and subdual tactics (page 23) can help good fighters do their best.

PALADINS

No other class shows the power and might of strictly adhering to the lawful good alignment like a paladin. In addition to a lengthy discussion of lawful good (page 6), new magic weapons (page 30) and new spells (page 28) help paladins further their goals.

ROGUES

Not always connected with a good alignment in people's minds, the rogue fits well as a good-hearted scoundrel. The *bondbreaker's boots* (page 30) and new rogue talents (page 25) are just some of the tools for good rogues.

WITCHES

Tapping into a mysterious source of arcane power, good witches have new patron themes (page 27), new spells (page 28), and new hexes (page 27) to help spread good in the world.

FOR EVERY CHARACTER

Certain game elements transcend the particulars of a character's race or class. The following elements detailed in this book work equally well for any character used in the Pathfinder Roleplaying Game, regardless of focus, type, or background.

PHILOSOPHIES

Presented as a way to help players better understand the nuances of the various good alignments, this section provides ideas for good characters' backgrounds and motivations as they begin adventuring (page 4).

GOOD ALIGNMENTS

Not just for clerics and paladins, these sections break down the three good alignments for all characters. Each provides philosophical concepts for playing in that alignment, advantages and challenges a character might expect to encounter, and traits that complement that alignment (pages 6–11).

REDEMPTION

Not every enemy is best dealt with through wholesale slaughter. Some villains may be beyond redemption, but others can be led into the light by good-hearted characters with righteous goals (page 18).

BAD SITUATIONS

Sometimes good characters have to struggle to be good in the face of personal conflicts and sometimes good characters find their origins in some of the darker places on Golarion. This section helps players see the value of conflict (page 14).

❓ QUESTIONS TO ASK YOUR GM

Asking your GM the following questions can help you to get the most out of *Pathfinder Player Companion: Champions of Purity*.

❶ How strict are we going to be about alignment? What are the penalties for deviating from it?

❷ If I am playing a paladin, how closely do I need to follow my paladin's code?

❸ What are the chances we will get to take enemies alive? Will we have a chance to redeem foes once we've captured them?

OTHER RULES ELEMENTS

In addition to the rules elements listed on the facing page, this book provides the following new rules for specific classes.

FOR CASTING CLASSES

FOR MARTIAL CLASSES

FOR SKILLED CLASSES

DID YOU KNOW?

Tim Nightengale, founder of PaizoCon and friend of Paizo, plays a paladin of Abadar (inspired by Jim Backus) named Howell B. Talbot III in James Jacobs's long-running office campaign.

RULES INDEX

The following feats, magic items, traits, and spells are presented in this Player Companion.

Why be good? It's a question that often goes unanswered in fantasy roleplaying games like Pathfinder. Why is that so? Because lucre and level advancement in many such games tend to be rewards for defeating evil. Though the player characters loot treasure vaults and murder monsters, they are heroes struggling against a rising tide of darkness. Playing such characters allows us to satisfy that inherent desire in all of us to rise above the evil of our world and champion something positive, much like superheroes or our favorite characters from fantasy literature do.

The world of Golarion abounds with opportunities to join epic struggles against evil. Characters can take up with the Mendevian Crusaders in the ongoing battle to extinguish the demonic tide flooding the lands and stop the Worldwound's expansion; they can tangle with the undead of Geb, freeing pockets of humans from the vile rulers who use the living as chattel; or they can aid Andoran in its efforts to annihilate the slave trade. Other possibilities include freeing the frozen land of Irrisen from the Witch Queen Baba Yaga or overthrowing the Midnight Lord's hold on Nidal.

Playing good characters is certainly challenging in any game world, especially when the game's trappings—level advancement, ability gains, and fantastic magical items and artifacts—are so exciting that they can sometimes distract you from your character's noble aims and purpose, thereby separating you from the game's true spirit. While leveling up by slaying monsters is part of play, and gaining cool magical items does make your character more difficult to defeat, the heart of the game is about players coming together in common cause in the face of nigh-overwhelming evil.

So what is the real reward of playing a good character? It is beating back the insurgent forces of darkness, saving a small town from being overrun by undead, and building a bastion of safety in the chaotic wilderness to serve as a front line against invading hordes. It is saving the day, defeating evil, and gaining the gratitude of a helpless village. Such are the real rewards of true heroes.

Use the following motivations to help focus your character's purpose in the game and build your champion into a world-renowned hero. Then consult the appropriate alignment section in the pages that follow to see how you can differentiate your character from other individuals of the same alignment.

MOTIVATIONS FOR GOOD CHARACTERS

If you want to take on the role of a good character, you can make your job easier by planting a strong motivation at your character's core. The following ideals can help define your good character's personality and guide her actions.

Equality: No individual is better than any other. You strongly support the philosophies of the Galtans Jubannich and Hosetter, who advocated the inalienable rights of the common folk and inspired revolts against the established order in Galt and Andoran. The People's

Revolt in Andoran epitomizes this philosophy, and you may actually be a citizen of Andoran (or Galt). Or perhaps tales of the successful revolt and insight into the philosophers' teachings have captured your heart and mind, rousing you to fight for the civil rights of others.

Freedom: People are meant to be free. Nothing incites your ire like witnessing slavers buy and sell others, hearing stories about raiders kidnapping people to bring them to market in other lands, or learning about leaders who subject their people to harsh treatment or impose severe restrictions on their people's liberties.

You abhor slavery in all its aspects, and seek to release the downtrodden from dictatorial rulers and eradicate the slave trade—or at least disrupt and curb it where you can. With this ideal, you might be from Andoran, the River Kingdoms, or Sargava.

Honor: The true measure of a person is her honor, how she responds and acts, whether in the midst of war or in everyday matters. You follow a strict code of behavior that guides your path in this world, and you expect others to do likewise. While your strong sense of honor may lead you to be a cavalier or paladin, you could just as easily be a wizard with a code of honor regarding magical duels—or maybe there is honor among thieves, and you are a rogue who regulates the thieves' guilds, ensuring only those who abuse the less fortunate with their excessive wealth are relieved of it. With this ideal, you might be from Lastwall, Mendev, or Taldor.

Justice: It is important to you that others receive the punishment they deserve for wrongdoings, and the law must be fair to all. You might fight to protect the civil rights accorded under the law, tangling with politicians who seek to disregard or outright abuse them. Or you might make it your goal to hunt down wanted individuals and groups, returning them to face their just punishment in a court of law. You insist on capturing such individuals and bringing them to justice, though you may also see yourself as the hand that metes out deserved punishments. With this ideal, you might be from the Five Kings Mountains, Lastwall, or Mendev.

Mercy: You believe all beings should be treated with compassion, even if they are transgressors. For instance, you would rather imprison a murderer than kill him outright for his crimes. Also, you do not believe in exterminating the offspring of wicked creatures when they are encountered, as you believe the innocent young should not be punished for the crimes of their elders. Instead, you might seek to find a place for them to be taken in. With this ideal, you may be from almost any region (including Katapesh, Qadira, and any part of Taldor), but you are likely a worshiper of Sarenrae, Shelyn, or Milani.

Order: Good can only be achieved through order, no matter what other philosophies espouse. In this regard, you might hold laws to be absolutely necessary for the good of all, and refuse to participate in actions that would bring you into conflict with the law. The law is black and white, so you brook no conversations regarding its spirit

GOOD ALIGNMENTS

Alignment is a tool to aid players in creating personalities for their characters. It is a guideline for a character's morality, and Game Masters should not use it to unduly hamper characters, nor should it be used to straitjacket PCs in regard to determining the relationships between them. Just because two characters are of good alignments—possibly the same alignment—does not guarantee they can work well together. Other personality traits ultimately affect the type of relationship formed, not just similarity along the good-evil alignment axis.

The good alignments are shorthand codes indicating that characters generally have some of the following characteristics: they oppose evil, respect life, defend the innocent, and sometimes make personal sacrifices to aid others. In contrast, characters with evil alignments have no qualms about killing innocents and sacrificing others as a means to achieving their own goals.

The alignment rules are indeed part of the game, and they should not be ignored, but they need not spoil your fun. GMs and players should discuss alignment's role in the campaign, making sure that all agree or understand how the system works within the game, how much alignment will be stressed, and what its ultimate role is in the game. In such conversations, your GM may want to provide a procedure for changing or deviating from an alignment and for any character effects that might result from doing so, particularly in regard to paladins or monks.

The following pages present several examples of each of the good alignments, showing that characters need not be cookie-cutter versions of each other but rather can include a variety of opportunities for roleplaying. Additionally, they detail significant advantages and challenges for each of the alignments, while discussing character possibilities and ways to deal with moral quandaries.

versus its actual text. Or perhaps you believe one's own daily life should be planned and controlled to the tiniest detail—you have your daily rituals, and these cannot be disrupted. Order in life leads to a clear, peaceful mind. With this ideal, you might be from Druma, the Five Kings Mountains, Lastwall, Mendev, Molthune, or Rahadoum.

Security/Safety: You grew up in a contended area, and you learned early on that security and safety were paramount to your community. You have dedicated yourself to ensuring and defending the safety of others ever since. In addition to protecting them in times of need, you might help train a village's militia, assist in building walls, and provide tactical advice to leaders of such communities.

With this ideal, you might be from Mendev, defending the lands against the demon infestation, or from Lastwall, where you keep the tides of Belkzen orcs from overrunning your homeland. You might also be from Isger, the Lands of the Linnorm Kings, the Mwangi Expanse, Nirmathas, the Sodden Lands, or Ustalav.

Lawful Good

Lawful good characters regard law as necessary for the welfare of society. They fight to abolish or change laws they deem unjust, and they always aid those in need. Lawful good characters strive to be forthright in their words and deeds, refuse to lie to others, and keep their covenants. They oppose evil wherever it is found, and avoid putting the good of the individual ahead of what is good for the masses. For these characters, the end rarely justifies the means. Characters drawn to honor, righting wrongs, or making sacrifices for others might be attracted to this alignment.

PHILOSOPHIES

Lawful good characters vary widely, especially in terms of their zeal for their beliefs. Some may be fanatical examples of the alignment, while others apply these ideals more loosely in their lives. The following examples showcase just a few of the possible approaches to this alignment.

BUILDERS

Builder characters believe in the importance of close-knit families and strong communities, and they teach others to be self-sufficient. Builders revere order and law, regarding these concepts as the answer to all of civilization's problems; for them, a strong, benevolent government is what allows civilizations to thrive. Builders often assist in creating actual structures and items as a part of community's attempt to improve members' quality of life.

If you are a builder, you:
- Strive for order and organization.
- View strong government as necessary for civilization's cultivation, and strong families and communities as the building blocks of successful settlements.
- Use your creativity and skills to teach others how to improve their lives and communities, and gladly offer your assistance when others are moved to create order and structure.

Code: You bring order to society through your creations, whether material or philosophical.

CRUSADERS

Crusaders endeavor to stamp out the presence of evil wherever it arises. These just, strong individuals spend their lives in pursuit of such heroic endeavors, tenaciously taking the fight to the root of evil in an attempt to eradicate it. Crusaders seek honor, valor, and glory in their pursuit of evil, and willingly sacrifice themselves in their efforts to destroy their targets. Many crusader types follow Iomedae, the Sword of Light.

If you are a crusader, you:
- Abhor evil in all its aspects.
- Are motivated to right wrongs and to stamp out evil and injustice.
- Seek honor and glory through your actions, and suffer death over accepting dishonor.

Code: You are honorable and risk your life to eradicate the evil threatening your lands or the lives of those you've vowed to protect.

GUARDIANS

Guardians respect life and believe there is no greater duty or higher calling than protecting the lives of innocents and those who are too venerable to protect themselves. These brave, unwavering individuals gladly risk life and limb in defending whoever or whatever they have vowed to protect, whether it's a city, village, fortress wall, or even a strategic pass. They willingly sacrifice themselves to the last soul to carry out their duty, and they find their honor, valor, and glory in defense rather than in taking the battle to others. When not actively involved in protecting their charge, they spend their time teaching defensive tactics and skills to those willing to learn.

If you are a guardian, you:
- Protect the lives of others at your own risk.
- Are motivated to protect the weak and the innocent.
- Improve the tactics and defensive skills of those you aid.

Code: You risk your life to protect the lives and well-being of others.

ADVANTAGES AND CHALLENGES

Lawful good characters are proficient at understanding bureaucracies, following laws, and cultivating order and structure in their own lives and in others'. They are naturally helpful, and others find them trustworthy, even if they don't share the same alignment. Additionally, lawful good characters are adept at deciding which actions are lawful and benefit society rather than the individual. With their focus on order, they can often build governmental stability where none previously existed.

These characters sometimes have problems defying laws, even when the laws are unjust. Instead of disobeying or protesting against such laws, they work within the provided structure or system to change those laws, and they implore others to do so as well. They feel guilty lying to others, even if only asked to fib to provide a ruse for their companions. Similarly, they won't break the law to help good-intentioned party members perform actions that might have beneficial results.

When they're adventuring in urban areas with their companions, lawful good characters may feel compelled to excuse themselves from certain plans or attempt to reason with those more lenient in their interpretation of the law. It's much easier for lawful good characters to ignore the bad behavior of other party members when exploring ruins and wilderness areas outside the direct jurisdiction of a governing body.

OPPORTUNITIES AND ALLIES

The character class most often associated with the lawful good alignment is the paladin, but this alignment may also include monks, who are always lawful—in fact, monks who take levels in the champions of Irori prestige class must be lawful good. With a few exceptions, the other character classes allow for any alignment. However, playing a lawful good rogue—though feasible via the game's rules—may be challenging. Such a character would, however, be a good addition to a law enforcement body as an investigator, or might travel as a scout or spy for a military or knightly order. She might also be a trustworthy appropriator of treasures lost in the depths of old ruins.

In the Inner Sea region, lawful good characters can find plenty of opportunities to adventure and find allies. These characters may be specifically interested in lending their support to the following organizations.

Knightly Orders: Knightly orders suiting this alignment can be found among the crusaders of Mendev, who struggle to stem the teeming Worldwound's demonic invaders, as well as in Lastwall's Knights of Ozem, who concentrate their efforts on the orc hordes of Belkzen and maintaining their sacred duty of guarding against the Whispering Tyrant's return. The Eagle Knights of Andoran, who stamp out slavery and promote the ideals of Andoran, constitute another organization lawful good characters may wish to ally with or join.

Lawful Nations: Aiding the lawful nations of Mendev and Lastwall, whether working with or without the nations' famous knightly orders, could interest characters of this alignment. And in Tian Xia, lawful good characters may wish to defend Zi Ha and Jinin against rampaging giants, hobgoblins, and oni. After all, if these nations fall, it's only a matter of time before the invaders threaten other regions.

Social Order: Bringing peace and order to a community or nation should be a paramount ideal to a lawful good character. Settling conflict and establishing a fair body of laws may be more often associated with politicians, legislators, and barristers, but an adventurer can pursue those ideals as well. Whether she focuses on keeping the peace or fighting against those who seek to upset the traditions of a particular society, an adventurer in an urban environment can instill the principles of a lawful good alignment in its people.

TRAITS

The following traits complement characters of lawful good alignment.

Blessed Touch (Faith): You may have been raised in a devout family, studied the divine in a formal church environment, or even learned how to combine traditional healing techniques with those of divine casters. In so doing, you have focused yourself into being the perfect vessel for your deity. Divine power flows through you like a mountain stream, making your healing touch more potent than that of others. You heal 1 additional point of damage when using lay on hands, channeling energy, or casting a cure spell.

Hard to Kill (Combat): Your strong will to live and spread good combined with your pure physicality makes you a tough opponent to take down. You may have discovered this as a child after a tragic accident or during the course of your first battle. When you are attempting a Constitution check to stabilize when dying, the penalty on the check is only half your negative hit point total instead of your full negative hit point total.

Weapon of Peace (Combat): Even though you are a trained combatant, proficient with any number of weapons, you don't relish killing your enemies. It's not that you're afraid of seeing blood, but rather that disabling a foe is superior to killing someone capable of admitting defeat. When using a melee weapon that deals lethal damage to instead deal nonlethal damage, you take only a –2 penalty instead of –4.

Neutral Good

Neutral good characters can see both sides of the lawful-chaotic axis, understanding that some choices are indeed better for all, and others are better for individuals. Because supporting either extreme on the axis does not motivate them, neutral good characters are often considered the "true good" alignment. They seek to do the most good in the world to make it a better place and to help others when possible. Neither anarchy nor the need for strict order concerns them. Neutral good characters support laws that benefit all, but have no qualms about ignoring unjust laws or tyrannical rulers.

PHILOSOPHIES

Neutral good characters vary widely, especially in terms of their zeal for their beliefs. Some may be fanatical examples of the alignment, while others apply these ideals more loosely in their lives. They find slavery, whether legal or not, abhorrent, and may make it their goal to destroy such institutions wherever they find them. The following examples showcase just a few of the possible approaches to this alignment.

HEALERS

Healers value life, seeing beauty and good in all living creatures. Healers offer their curative powers to those in need, regardless of their patients' alignment, believing it's their duty to use their skills and magic to maintain the purity of life itself. As life is all-important to them, they take oaths never to do harm to others or to take lives; when forced to fight, they protect themselves, but tend to employ abilities that hamper or entrap their enemies rather than killing them outright. After all, every being's life is important to the universe, and the loss of any soul is a true tragedy to healers.

If you are a healer, you:
- Value life above all else.
- Use your curative knowledge and abilities to heal the sick and wounded.
- Fight defensively, and only to capture or weaken opponents.

Code: You seek to maintain the life and health of others, and do not take others' lives.

MEDIATORS

It is not possible for all members of a community to have their way; life is all about compromise, and mediators specialize in steering rational individuals to agreeable terms and favorable outcomes. When things go badly or they must deal with hostile people, mediators do not rashly pull their weapons on others, but instead offer alternative options for resolution through diplomacy or intimidation. Of course, many creatures lack enlightenment, and thus don't accept compromise. When words fall on deaf ears, mediators resort to weapons to win the day.

If you are a mediator, you:
- Value balance and peaceful, beneficial resolutions.
- Are motivated by the desire to keep the peace and diffuse conflict.
- Attempt to use your wisdom and charisma when dealing with nonevil creatures.

Code: When conflict arises between reasonable creatures of either axis of your alignment, you offer your diplomatic skills to accomplish compromise or agreement.

REDEEMERS

Redeemers believe that with a few exceptions, most beings are capable of goodness. Beings not following the path of light need only be given a chance to renounce their wayward behavior and be enlightened to the true path of goodness, thus allowing them to redeem their souls and atone for their vile deeds. Redeemers believe in patience, knowing old habits are hard to break. Of course, those who refuse proffered redemption opportunities must not be allowed to continue along their destructive paths, so redeemers must permanently prevent them from doing further harm.

If you are a redeemer, you:
- Value life and are patient.
- Are motivated to bring others into the light, believing they deserve a second chance.
- Are willing to kill those who refuse redemption.

Code: The lost can be returned to the light if given the chance; you must offer it and show them the way.

ADVANTAGES AND CHALLENGES

Neutral good characters excel at seeing both sides of a situation, and they use this ability to inform their actions, doing what they believe will produce the most good. These characters seek balance and harmony in their dealings with others; they know to avoid conversations leading to heated topics, and keep their responses to the middle of the road. They understand the value of nature, and realize that expanding civilization into the wilderness is not always the most appropriate thing to do.

Because of their ability to see all facets of a situation, neutral good characters can sometimes have difficulty in choosing a side between other good beings. For this reason, others may label them as wishy-washy or not capable of serious conviction.

Dealing with other characters aligned along the lawful-chaotic axis can also be challenging, especially in mixed-alignment adventuring groups. The neutral good characters will not always agree with the lawful good characters' meticulous need to plan their actions, control others, or prevent others from disobeying laws that interfere with the party's goals—sometimes less-than-honest tactics are necessary, after all. Conversely, neutral good characters might find chaotic good characters a little on the uncontrollable side, not liking the wild bent of their ideas or actions. Too much freedom of thought and action, they believe, just makes one irresponsible.

Neutral good characters give great consideration to their actions before deeming them correct; some neutral good characters find it unfathomable that others cannot see their viewpoint as the most sensible.

OPPORTUNITIES AND ALLIES

Neutral good is an alignment common to the druid class, who must select any neutral alignment. Neutral good serves as an effective alignment for most any class, except the monk and paladin, who must be lawful.

Exploration and Preservation: The neutral frontier lands of Varisia can hold significant interest for characters of this alignment. This fast-growing area is a great stepping-stone for characters wanting to do good, preserve beautiful works of art and history, and make names for themselves. Sandpoint makes a wonderful hometown for beginning good characters, and Magnimar is especially welcoming toward rising stars. Preservationists may also want to enter Galt to retrieve its relics and artifacts before the revolutionaries ravage them all, or might join the people of the Mwangi Expanse in their struggle against the depredations of the demon-worshipping Gorilla King and exploitation by would-be colonizers and treasure hunters.

Freedom Fighting and Andoran: Neutral good characters may hail from Andoran or gain allies in Andoran's Eagle Knights, and they may find the kingdom's political views and ideals of freedom from slavery and tyranny particularly appealing. Neutral good characters might involve themselves in the fight to free slaves, and their assistance would be greatly welcomed. They might also join the organization, climbing its ranks as they gain experience and levels.

Peace, Redemption, and Refuge: Neutral good characters, especially servants of Sarenrae, might find Golarion's hotbeds of chaos ripe for intervention in the form of redemption and mediation. Such realms include Brevoy, where nobles war against each other for control; Galt, the blood-soaked land of revolution; Numeria, the dark-mage-run land of super science; the River Kingdoms, the land of mercenaries and bandits; Sargava, an oppressive former colony on the verge of rebellion; and the treacherous pirate isles of the Shackles. Mediators and redeemers could bring calm to these regions, and could even form their own refuge for redeemed souls.

TRAITS

The following traits complement characters of neutral good alignment.

Helpful (Combat): You always know the best way to assist your companions, be it assisting them with a task, defending them in battle, or helping them place a well-aimed strike. When using the aid another action, you grant your ally a +3 bonus instead of a +2 bonus.

Mediator (Social): You have a way with calming tempers, using cool logic to sooth heated disagreements, and you were always the one to settle arguments among your friends, family, and community. You receive a +1 trait bonus on Diplomacy checks. In addition, you receive a +1 trait bonus to the DC of any charm or compulsion effect that does not provide ongoing control and results in peaceful acts, such as *calm emotions*, *sleep*, or a *suggestion* to lay down arms.

Redeemer (Faith): You've always held the strong belief that morality is everyone's choice, and that those who act in wicked ways have simply never been shown how their actions truly affect others. If they could be shown their errors, then they would accept a more positive course of action—and you have just enough patience to see this through. When acting as a sponsor for an evil creature seeking redemption (see page 18), your patience and kindness grant the creature a +3 bonus on its save rather than a +1 bonus.

Chaotic Good

Chaotic good characters are strong-willed and self-directed—masters of their own destiny. They act as their consciences dictate, viewing the plights of the weak and innocent with compassion and correcting injustices when they can. Chaotic good characters disregard others' expectations of their behavior, finding many laws and regulations too limiting to their personal freedom. They resent those who inflict their ideals on others, especially through intimidation, and are often reluctant to conform. Chaotic good characters want the freedom to do as they will and desire others to be free of oppression as well.

PHILOSOPHIES

Chaotic good characters vary widely, especially in terms of their zeal for their beliefs. Some chaotic good characters seem to be fanatical examples of their alignment, while others apply these ideals more loosely in their lives. These carefree souls follow their own whims and pleasures, harming no one unless their personal sense of justice is inflamed. They find slavery an utter abomination, and fight against all instances of it they encounter. The following examples showcase just a few of the possible approaches to this alignment.

ACTIVISTS

Activists ensure others question and reflect upon the origin of beliefs and knowledge, both their own and that of others. They do not do so out of malice or a desire to disrupt others' thoughts, but rather out of a duty to help others realize their true selves—a person cannot truly be a free person until her thoughts and beliefs are, in fact, her own, not the rote drivel instilled by those wanting a society of faithful sheep.

If you are an activist, you:
- Value questioning the establishment.
- Are motivated to "awaken" other free thinkers.
- Are a seeker of knowledge and truth.
- Live life without restricting others.

Code: You want others to question what they know, ensuring each individual is truly living honestly and thinking for himself.

FREEDOM FIGHTERS

Freedom fighters believe no one should suffer the indignity of slavery or be forced to serve a government that rejects or ignores the rights of its people. Everyone is born free and should remain so. Liberty is the right of all, and tyrants and slavers must be thwarted or eradicated by any means necessary. Freedom fighters spread their ideals in hopes of inspiring others to wage war against slavers and oppressors. Although liberty is an ideal rooted in neutral good Andoran, many of its freedom fighters are chaotic good.

If you are a freedom fighter, you:
- Value freedom and liberty for all.
- Are motivated to eradicate slavery.
- Ensure laws do not restrict individuals' rights.

Code: You find tyranny and slavery the most intolerable crimes in existence, and you long to free every man, woman, and child from their grip.

VIGILANTES

Vigilantes believe those individuals enforcing the laws of the land are too lazy or uncaring to effectively punish evildoers, or that their hands are tied by the law. Therefore, vigilantes step forward to deliver justice to wrongdoers, serving as both judge and punisher for thieves, thugs, and murderers. When their prey happens to be slavers or violent oppressors, vigilantes sometimes cross paths with freedom fighters. For vigilantes, justice must be delivered at all costs, and they risk their own lives to keep the lives of innocents safe and secure.

If you are a vigilante, you:
- Value the justice delivered by your own hand.
- Are motivated to punish evildoers.
- Disregard laws to bring about your own justice, and are, therefore, often a wanted individual.

Code: You risk limb and life to bring wrongdoers to justice for their crimes, and in doing so, make life better for others.

ADVANTAGES AND CHALLENGES

Chaotic good characters follow their own consciences and are adaptable, easily rolling with life's punches. They rarely make plans too far in advance, preferring to take a wait-and-see approach to most things, which allows them to adjust their actions or reactions in a single heartbeat. They have no qualms about breaking laws, especially when doing so will save others or protect others' rights from being trammeled.

Chaotic good characters want freedom for themselves and others, and find it difficult to live in societies they deem too restrictive to individuals. They view laws and regulations as unneeded mechanisms of control rather than protection. Deeply inherent in the chaotic good character's philosophy is the belief that most individuals are good and will do good if given the freedom to act as they please. In this regard, these benevolent, kind-hearted individuals can be viewed as the most idealistic of the good alignments. Other good characters call their live-and-let-live attitude overly idealistic, instead believing that individuals are more selfish than kindhearted in nature and need guidance to become good. The chaotic good philosophy, however, holds that because individuals are not all like-minded persons, imposing such guidance and laws to force them to conform to a single mold deforms their spirits, creating flaws and cracks where evil can more easily find a foothold.

While chaotic good characters do not accept that individuals must sacrifice their ideals and follow laws for the good of the whole, they willingly sacrifice themselves (and their individuality) to protect the whole in the name of good.

OPPORTUNITIES AND ALLIES

Chaotic good is not an alignment embedded in any particular character class, though it can be an excellent one for barbarian characters, who must avoid lawful alignments. The most difficult character class to portray with a chaotic good alignment might be the cavalier, as cavaliers are tied to teamwork by the nature of their combat skills and must follow an order as well. Such knights, however, could serve as effective freedom fighters and leaders in the fight for liberty.

Freedom Fighting (Patriots): Chaotic good characters might be very attracted to Andoran's philosophies in regard to liberty being a right inalienable to all. If they choose to join the fight against slavery, chaotic good characters could find allies in the Eagle Knights, though they might prefer to work outside the organization, as doing things their own way is deeply rooted in their nature. War-torn Nirmathas, a land also ruled by the ideals of freedom and self-sufficiency, is in need of defenders as well.

Freedom Fighting (Rebels): Chaotic good characters wishing to fight against tyranny can find opportunities to make a difference in the shadowy servitor state of Nidal; in Razmiran, the theocracy of the living god; in Geb, domain of the dead; in the diabolical empire of Cheliax; and in Sargava, a former colony bent on subjugating the native populace. These are all oppressive lands in need of heroes. The Eagle Knights are possible allies in these fights as well, and aiding the halfling Bellflower Network in freeing slaves from Cheliax and bringing them to Andoran is another possibility.

Racial Allies: Chaotic good characters might find allies among the elves and half-elves, with whom they share not only an alignment (generally speaking), but also a curiosity about life and a zeal to forge their own paths in the world. This tendency is even stronger in the case of half-elves, who often find themselves without a unified homeland and feel they must create their own destinies. Elves are more commonly found in the wilderness, making it reasonable that they could be useful allies for druid and ranger characters. Chaotic good characters might also find allies among aasimars who tend toward chaos, or perhaps even among the rare but free-willed catfolk.

TRAITS

The following traits complement characters of a chaotic good alignment.

Careful Combatant (Combat): You have a strong sense of self-preservation, believing it is more important to safely extract yourself from a fight that has turned hopeless than to stubbornly stand your ground and risk death—for when you're dead, you can't protect the innocent. When using the withdraw action, both the first and second squares of your movement are not considered threatened by any opponents you can see, rather than just the first square.

Hardly a Fool (Social): You have always been able to ferret out lies and deception. Maybe you worked as an investigator for a time, you came from a place rife with lies, or you've studied the human condition long enough to read a person's face and get to the heart of his message. You gain a +1 trait bonus on Sense Motive checks and a +1 trait bonus on saving throws against illusion effects.

Spark of Creation (Magic): You have always had a knack for making useful things, and your talent as an artisan was evident even at an early age. You gain a +1 trait bonus on Craft checks, and the cost of creating magic items is reduced by 5%.

Paragons of Virtue

Good-aligned characters seek allies who have outlooks similar to their own, and though many regions of Golarion struggle daily under the yoke of evil overlords, several bastions of goodness thrive in the world. The following section provides an overview of good races and organizations that players can use in the backgrounds of their good characters, and that can lend good characters support in their battles. This section also details several homelands and four new traits suitable for good characters, each providing a starting point for adventure.

GOOD-ALIGNED RACES

Players may select the races of their good characters from those detailed in the *Pathfinder RPG Core Rulebook* or (with GM approval) from the expanded list of races in the *Pathfinder RPG Advanced Race Guide*. Some races are more disposed toward goodness than others, and though characters from these races can technically be of any alignment, they tend to be good.

Aasimars: Aasimars, who are more fully detailed in *Pathfinder Player Companion: Blood of Angels*, have inherited traits from angels and other good-aligned outsiders. Their celestial ancestry heavily inclines them toward the cleric, oracle, and paladin classes, though bards, inquisitors, sorcerers, and summoners also appear among their ranks.

Catfolk: Adaptable and eager to explore, catfolk tend toward good alignments, often with an element of chaos. As natural trackers comfortable in the wild, many catfolk become druids or rangers, and given their love of performance and desire to be the center of attention, bards, monks, and sorcerers are also common among their kind.

Elves and Half-Elves: Both races have a natural grace and a connection to nature, and tend toward a chaotic good alignment. Suitable for any character class, elves and half-elves frequently make the best of their racial abilities, keen senses, and natural penchant for magic and elegant combat.

Samsarans: These reincarnated beings lean toward a lawful good alignment and are deeply spiritual. Samsarans favor the cleric, monk, oracle, and paladin classes.

GOOD-ALIGNED ORGANIZATIONS

Good characters may approach, and possibly join, the following organizations to gain support in their endeavors.

Knights: Many orders of knights exist throughout the Inner Sea, including the Eagle Knights, the Knights of Ozem, and the Mendevian Crusaders. Devotees of freedom, justice, and liberty, the Eagle Knights of Andoran fight pirates and slavers, undermining the trafficking of slaves throughout the Inner Sea. From Vigil, the Knights of Ozem maintain watch over the Whispering Tyrant's prison, while simultaneously keeping Lastwall safe from Ustalav's encroaching undead and Belkzen's invading orc hordes. The Mendevian Crusaders organize strategic strikes against the demons of the Worldwound, protect their homeland's borders from evil, and relentlessly eradicate internal bastions of demon worshipers and demonic allies through their purifying inquisitions. For more information on these knightly organizations, see *Pathfinder Campaign Setting: The Inner Sea World Guide* and *Pathfinder Player Companion: Knights of the Inner Sea*.

Racial Organizations: Other good organizations that characters may seek aid from or join include the Bellflower Network, a group of halfling emancipators; the Lantern Bearers, a secretive organization of elven slayers dedicated to eradicating the drow; and the Ninth Battalion, dwarven warriors dedicated to defending their race. More information about these organizations can be found in *Pathfinder Campaign Setting: Faction Guide.*

Challenging Organizations: There are a number of other organizations that don't require a good alignment for membership, but don't exclude good characters from joining. Interacting with some of these might present more of a challenge for a good character, while others are easy to work within. Joining the Hellknights might not strike a good character as an appropriate career choice, but there is nothing to stop a lawful good character from doing so. Riftwardens, who seek to protect planar boundaries and fight against the Blackfire Adepts, require their membership to be nonevil. Finally, while the Pathfinder Society is generally considered to be a neutral organization, the group performs many good deeds throughout the Inner Sea. See *The Inner Sea World Guide*, the *Faction Guide*, and *Pathfinder Campaign Setting: Paths of Prestige* for more information on these groups.

GOOD-ALIGNED HOMELANDS

Good-aligned characters may hail from anywhere across Golarion, but certain good-aligned regions tend to produce more virtuous, idealistic, and heroic characters than others.

Whether from the vast coastal cities of Almas or Augustana or smaller towns like Alvis or Falcon's Hollow, characters from Andoran, the birthplace of freedom, believe all persons should be free from the yoke of tyrannical rulers and the bonds of slavery. Abolitionists are rife in Andoran, and characters from Almas may be actively involved in disrupting the slave trade throughout the Inner Sea.

In northeastern Avistan, the crusading theocracy of Mendev fights a never-ending battle against the demons of the Worldwound. Mendevian characters remain ever-vigilant against both the overt and subtle infiltration of evil into their region, and many combine their crusading temperament with a strong faith in Iomedae, former servant of Aroden and the original leader of the Knights of Ozem against the Whispering Tyrant. Those from the city of Kenabres could follow the zealous prophet Hulrun, aiding his inquisitions against demon worshipers and helping purify (often by fire) the demon-tainted among them.

Characters from the heavily forested Nirmathas have a deep-seated independent streak, having lived under the heavy bureaucratic rule of Cheliax and then Molthune for some time. Freedom is a great motivating factor for these characters, all of whom hold liberty and self-sufficiency as the greatest of ideals. The Chernasardo rangers epitomize the undying spirit inherent in those from Nirmathas, as they strive daily to keep the forest free of invaders.

Good characters also actively campaign in many other areas across Golarion. Good characters could likely come from the cities of Iadara (if elven) or Greengold (if human) in Kyonin (CG), the battle-tested region of Lastwall (LG), the scholarly city of Nantambu in the Mwangi Expanse (NG), or the goblin-harried city of Sandpoint (NG) in

PRESTIGE CLASSES FOR GOOD CHARACTERS
The following prestige classes require a good alignment: Bellflower tiller, champion of Irori, Golden Legionnaire, Lantern Bearer, Magaambyan arcanist (*Pathfinder Campaign Setting: Paths of Prestige*); Inheritor's crusade (*Pathfinder Adventure Path #26*); and Steel Falcon (*Pathfinder Player Companion: Andoran, Spirit of Liberty*).

The following prestige classes don't require a good alignment, but do require worship of Sarenrae and Iomedae, respectively: Dawnflower dissident and Knight of Ozem (*Paths of Prestige*).

Varisia. Characters hailing from Tian Xia might come from Hwanggot, a peaceful holdout against imperialistic expansion (NG); the elven shogunate of Jinin (LG); the Abyss-threatened nation of Tianjing (NG), home to many aasimars; or Zi Ha (LG), a network of samsaran cities built atop monster-infested mountains (see *Pathfinder Player Companion: Dragon Empires Primer*).

GOOD TRAITS

The following traits suit characters of good alignment.

Affable (Social): You have a genial personality and make it a point to befriend and help people wherever you go. In your travels, you stop to aid others, tell interesting stories, and often buy rounds of drinks for patrons at the local taverns. You bring good cheer to those you encounter, and for this reason, you often find yourself attending important events or fruitful gatherings, and have even become an honorary member of many families. People find you trustworthy, and they are willing to share information with you. You gain a +2 trait bonus on Diplomacy checks to gather information, and can do so in half the normal time. In addition, Diplomacy and Knowledge (local) are always class skills for you.

Chosen of Iomedae (Faith): At your birth, your parents dedicated your soul to Iomedae to mold into a sword of her light. The goddess blessed you, granting you a gift of light to brighten your path through darkness and a fine sword with which to spread her will. You may cast *light* once per day as a spell-like ability (caster level 1st), and you begin play with a masterwork longsword. In addition, whenever *light* is cast upon this sword, the radius of *light* and its duration is doubled.

Demon Smiter (Combat): You grew up around those who fight the demons streaming out of the Worldwound, and from their stories you learned about the demons' weaknesses. You are likely from Mendev or have joined that nation's cause as a crusader. Once per day when fighting demons, you gain a +4 trait bonus on a single attack roll.

Transmuter of Korada (Magic): You learned the secrets of transmutation from a follower of the empyreal lord Korada. Whenever you cast a spell from the transmutation school, its effects manifest at +1 caster level. Additionally, select one of the following transmutation spells: *bear's endurance, bull's strength, cat's grace, eagle's splendor, fox's cunning,* or *owl's wisdom.* Once per day when you cast that spell, its duration is doubled. A spell affected by this trait cannot be modified further by the Extend Spell metamagic feat or similar abilities.

Good Characters in Bad Situations

In many games, playing good characters is the norm. However, some GMs like to interject ethical quandaries into the game from time to time to keep players on their toes and to test their characters' resolve—and because real life isn't always so cut and dry, why should your fantasy campaign be? This section presents a few topics that often rear their heads during the course of play as elements for your consideration. You may want to discuss some of the following quandaries with your GM and other players. This will allow you to see where everyone stands in regard to the idea of alignment.

ETHICS FOR ADVENTURERS

If complicated ethics that challenge a character's concept or force her to make difficult moral decisions is an element of play you would rather avoid, discussing this with your GM is important. It makes for a better game when everyone knows the expected boundaries in terms of what is considered fun. Some players, in fact, do not want to have anything that too closely resembles real life appearing in their fantasy games! Decide together what your group considers to be fair game.

One of the many quandaries good-aligned characters face during their adventuring careers is what to do about the progeny of evil humanoids. For example, shortly into their adventures, an adventuring party encounters a group of goblins who have been raiding a village, leaving a swath of death and destruction in their wake. The PCs track them to some caves and kill them—but the dead goblins leave behind babies. What should the PCs do with those? Kill them? Leave them be? What is the best and most appropriate thing for a good character to do in this situation?

Just as there are varying good alignments, there are different solutions to this problem. One good character might believe the children are not inherently evil, that their behavior is learned, and round up the young ones to take them to a higher power like a church, a monastery, or an orphanage set up to deal with the issue of raising humanoid children. Alternatively, he might decide to raise them himself! This could be viewed as the most saintly thing to do. Another character might decide not to do anything, leaving the children to the whims of nature—either the children will survive in the wild on their own, or they will not. Lastly, a good character who believes the younglings can never overcome their innate evil might kill them all outright, viewing the action as good, just, and the most merciful option.

Another quandary might be the presence of a party member or strong, supporting ally who is actually evil. For instance, can the party's paladin continue to work with the evil wizard in the group, or is it morally wrong to do so? This situation would certainly disquiet the paladin, but rather than refusing to work with the wizard, she could insist on trying to reform the person, who must surely have some ounce of goodness in him if he continues to aid the group. It might become her goal to bring this individual to the light, and she could work tirelessly to make it happen.

Non-paladin members of the group, depending upon their fervor toward goodness, might choose to ignore the issue entirely, unless the evil character does something overtly harmful to the group or an innocent person. Otherwise, they might accept him more as "neutral" until he shows his true colors, whether or not a detection of his true alignment indicates otherwise.

ALIGNMENT ON GOLARION

The Pathfinder RPG assumes good and evil are definitive things. Evidence for this outlook can be found in the indicated good or evil monster subtypes, spells that detect good and evil, and spells that have the good or evil descriptor. Characters using spells with the evil descriptor should consider themselves to be committing minor acts of evil, though using spells to create undead is an even more grievous act of evil that requires atonement.

Creatures with an evil subtype (generally outsiders) are creatures that are fundamentally evil: devils, daemons, and demons, for instance. Their redemption is rare, if it is even possible. They are evil to their very core, and commit evil acts perpetually and persistently. Mortals with an evil alignment, however, are different from these beings. In fact, having an evil alignment alone does not make one a supervillain or even require one to be thwarted or killed. The extent of a character's evil alignment might be a lesser evil, like selfishness, greed, or extreme vanity. Having these qualities might not even cause the character to detect as evil when subjected to *detect evil*, as creatures possessing 4 or fewer Hit Dice do not register to the spell (with the exception of clerics or other characters that radiate an aura).

GOOD CHARACTERS FROM BAD PLACES

Nations in the Inner Sea region run the gamut from benevolent fledgling democracies to brutal and tyrannical dictatorships. Characters can find their origins in any of these nations, and while it often makes sense for a good character to come from one of the more virtuous countries, it's equally reasonable that a good character was born in a bad place. Growing up in conflict with your homeland can lead to interesting situations and provide a compelling background for a good character, particularly one driven to bring good into the world and improve the situations of oppressed or tormented fellow citizens. Below are some of the nations in the Inner Sea region that are, on average, evil.

Cheliax: People throughout the Inner Sea are aware that this dwindling empire consorts with devils and uses those creatures to bring power to the country. Good characters from Cheliax can focus on leading a resistance against House Thrune, subverting the slave trade within their home country, or even disrupting policies of expansionism and exploitation in Cheliax's colonial holdings.

Geb: Ruled by undead and evil spellcasters, this nation uses zombies and slaves as its workforce to produce the food it trades with neighboring countries. Though the nation is overrun with undead, it still has plenty of mortal citizens and the place is relatively safe provided they keep their heads down and avoid attracting official

attention. Characters from Geb could grow up to be undead slayers, using knowledge of how undead operate to their advantage throughout their adventures.

Irrisen: This frozen nation is ruled by generations of witches, all cruel and cunning. Life in Irrisen is hard for its citizens, and its rulers are as harsh and cold as the persistent weather. Good characters from Irrisen could be members of the Heralds of Summer's Return, an underground resistance movement with its sights set on tearing down the monarchy and returning the nation to normal.

Nidal: This shadowy theocracy keeps its people under the thumb of the Umbral Court, creating a nation of thralls to the Midnight Lord. Total obedience is expected of all citizens, and a good character from Nidal might find herself banding with secret worshipers of Desna in their quest to drive back the oppressive shadow blanketing the land.

Razmiran: This theocracy led by a false god strictly rules its people with severe punishment and intimidation. Good characters raised in Razmiran have grown up under harsh and unjust laws, and may find themselves wanting to improve the quality of life for their families and fellow citizens. To achieve this, a character could ferret out secrets held by Razmir's trusted followers, subvert Razmir's erratic and cruel mandates, or even reveal the man for what he truly is.

Ustalav: This foggy land is steeped in horror. Tainted by the tyrannical evil of Tar-Baphon, Ustalav is now filled with secret agents of the lich-king seeking to return their lord to his prior power. Good characters from Ustalav can hunt down the evil that surrounds them on all sides.

Heavenly Virtues

Virtuous Creed

You accept a creed to guide your destiny toward good.

Prerequisite: You must be good.

Benefit: Select one of the following virtues. You must adhere to that virtue's creed in order to benefit from its bonus. If you break any part of the creed, you are unable to gain the benefits from that virtue for 24 hours. Significant violations require *atonement* for you to be able to benefit from this feat again.

Special: You can gain this feat multiple times. Each time you take this feat, you must choose a new virtue.

Humility

Creed: You must always show respect to others. You must put your own desires aside in favor of the needs of the masses. You must be conservative in dress and in actions, and wary not to display pride or gloat about your wealth or achievements.

Benefit: You add your Wisdom modifier on Diplomacy checks in addition to your Charisma modifier.

Courage

Creed: You can never willingly flee combat when others' lives are at risk. You must never show cowardice in sight of your enemies.

Benefit: When shaken, you gain a +3 bonus on Will saves against any effects that would worsen your condition to frightened or panicked.

Freedom

Creed: You must always seek to ensure that beings have the right to live their lives as their own. You must put an end to slavery when you see it, and break whatever chains hold others down, be they metaphysical or real.

Benefit: Once per day, you can reroll a Will save against a charm or compulsion effect and gain a +2 bonus on that reroll. You must decide to use this ability before the results are revealed. You must take the second roll, even if it is worse.

Purity

Creed: You must refrain from contact with unclean things and keep your thoughts unpolluted. You must not touch evil-aligned weapons or creatures. You must practice clean eating, ingesting only properly prepared foods that strengthen the body and mind.

Benefit: You gain a +2 bonus on all Fortitude saving throws against disease or poison. In addition, the onset time for any disease or poison is doubled.

Protection

Creed: You must always stand up for those weaker than yourself. You must defend your community against those that prey upon it.

Benefit: When you use the aid another action to improve an ally's AC against attacks, the bonus increases to +4 instead of +2.

Mercy

Creed: You must always accept an enemy's surrender. When your enemies are defeated in battle, you must attempt to stabilize them to the best of your ability. You must never bring undue suffering to those who are innocent.

Benefit: When using a weapon that deals lethal damage to instead deal nonlethal damage, you take no penalty on your attack roll.

Redemption

Changing alignment can be a tricky process, both in mechanical and roleplaying terms. Alignment shifts have little mechanical effect on characters of classes without alignment restrictions, so they can be as simple as the GM mentioning a drift one way or another. For some, though, redemption can be a driving force for character development or plots within a campaign. And for others, the desire to take a prestige or base class that requires characters to be good, or to use a good-aligned item, might encourage them to seek a purer path. This system presents guidelines for tracking a creature's path toward redemption. It allows for a great degree of customization and alteration to ensure it feels natural for players and fits comfortably into an ongoing campaign. But keep in mind that certain classes and other rules require a more demanding form of redemption, such as a paladin seeking atonement or a cleric or druid attempting to regain her spell powers. This system does not circumvent such requirements.

BECOMING GOOD

Each character has her own unique path to good. Many creatures are set in their ways and don't vacillate between distinct ethical philosophies, making such a fundamental change in thinking and acting an arduous road. The notion of good is as much about intention as it is about action. Simply committing a series of good acts is not enough to change a creature's alignment—it must want deep down within itself to be good. As such, finding true redemption

involves the creature passing through a number of stages on its path to goodness.

Intention: Determining a creature's intention is largely a roleplaying task. Creatures that truly seek redemption should display genuine remorse over evil acts they've committed and must be willing to embark on the difficult road to becoming good. If you are actively seeking to redeem a creature, there is no guarantee of success, but by offering it examples of mercy and decency you might spark a desire to do good in its heart. Many times, confessing one's past sins and evil deeds is the first step toward redemption. Purposefully completing at least one penance (see below) and succeeding at a Will save as outlined in the following rules should prove a creature is ready to begin its journey.

Calculating the Path to Good: To alter its alignment toward good, a creature must pass through a number of stages, depending on its starting alignment. A creature with an evil alignment must first shift its alignment to neutral before shifting its alignment to good. To make this shift, the creature must perform a number of penances equal to double its total Hit Dice. This number of penances must be completed for each stage of shift in alignment, from evil to neutral and again from neutral to good. If the creature seeking to become good gains additional Hit Dice or levels during the course of its redemption, the number of penances to be completed should reflect its new total Hit Dice.

For example, if a creature with a total of 7 Hit Dice completes 14 penances to shift from evil to neutral, but gains a level before completing its path from neutral to good, its total Hit Dice rise to 8 and it must now complete 16 penances in order to complete its path of redemption.

For exceptionally evil creatures, a GM may wish to increase the required number of penances to reflect a life of utter depravity. For creatures with the evil subtype, their alignment is ingrained into their very soul, and the GM may rule that they are beyond redemption of this sort or at the very least a difficult and exceptional series of tasks must be completed to facilitate the change in alignment.

Penances: To pass through each stage of its path to good, a creature must perform a number of good deeds equal to double its total Hit Dice. The GM decides exactly which penances are appropriate, but examples of such acts are included below.

When a creature completes the penances required for a stage, it must succeed at a Will save to overcome its nature. The DC of this save is equal to 10 + 1/2 the creature's total Hit Dice + its Charisma modifier.

If this save is successful, the penances have taken hold and the creature has completed another step toward becoming good. If the creature fails this save, it must complete another deed in order to gain a chance to attempt another save. It can continue to complete additional deeds after each failed save until it succeeds.

Sponsorship: It is far easier for a creature to change its alignment with the tutelage and support of another. Someone who wishes to become good can seek out the support of a good creature to improve its own chances of success. At each stage, a creature may enlist the help of a number of sponsors up to its Charisma modifier. Each sponsor aiding a creature on its path to redemption provides a +1 bonus on the creature's Will save (or saves, if the first save is unsuccessful) to complete that stage of its redemption.

To be a sponsor, a creature must absolutely believe in the penitent's ability and sincere intention to change its alignment. This certainty may arise from friendship, divine guidance, the application of divinations or mundane interrogation, or any other source that results in absolute conviction that the subject desires to be good.

Relapse: Each minor evil act a creature performs (casting spells with the evil descriptor, praying to an evil deity, using an evil magic device, mind controlling good creatures to commit evil acts, and so on) counts against whatever penances the character has already performed, effectively canceling one out. Any major evil act (knowingly slaying an innocent creature, spreading a disease among a community, inflicting pain on an innocent subject, or animating the dead) undoes all of the good work done for the current stage, and the creature must begin that stage anew. A GM may rule that a particularly heinous act reverses all work done, and shifts the creature back to its original evil alignment.

EXAMPLE PENANCES

The list that follows represents examples of penances that you can use to pursue redemption or assign to a penitent that you're sponsoring, with your GM's permission. Your GM should avoid presenting too may options for redemption at once, as doing so would allow you to choose the easiest penance over the one most appropriate to the situation—those who truly seek to repent shouldn't shy away from a good deed because it is difficult, expensive, or not their idea of fun. It is equally important, however, to work with your GM to ensure that penances are achievable, relevant, and available at a sufficient pace, so that the process of redemption doesn't interfere with the adventure and group dynamics. Getting this balance

right may be tricky, particularly if you are in a rush to become good.

- Confessing your past sins or evil acts to an appropriate good-aligned agent.
- Healing a creature you don't know from a disease, affliction, or poison when doing so gives you no personal advantage.
- Willingly submitting to a *geas/quest, mark of justice,* or similar spell to show you are committed enough to the process of redemption to risk harm if you fail.
- Casting a spell with the good descriptor. This penance can be completed only once per stage.
- Donating at least 50 gp to a good organization or faith. Each time you do so, the amount needed for the donation to qualify as a penance doubles.
- Sacrificing belongings gained through evil means.
- Freeing an oppressed, enslaved, or abused creature.
- Preaching a sermon of no less than 1 hour on the virtues of good behavior. This penance can only be completed once per week.
- Turning a creature that has committed a crime over to a good-aligned authority.
- Completing a task or quest for a good faith or organization without accepting payment. A GM may decide that a particularly challenging encounter may count as two or more penances.
- Fasting and praying for 12 hours (leading to fatigue).
- Creating a good item and giving it away for free.
- Showing mercy to a vanquished foe.
- Completing a task for a stranger and accepting no reward.
- Refraining from blasphemy or bad language in private or in conversation with others.
- Instructing other characters or NPCs in pure courses of action.
- Ignoring or not responding to insults or challenges from foes.
- Attempting a Diplomacy check to try and resolve a situation peaceably instead of resorting to combat.
- Refraining from lying or deception for an entire week.

Many other actions that may come up in play could be considered penances, and your GM should feel free to count such deeds when they occur. The process becomes much more natural and genuine if penitent characters seek out ways to be helpful and pure, rather than simply working their way through a set list.

Many powerful deities embody good ideals. Worshipers who draw power or conviction from these deities seek to do good in a variety of ways. This section presents these deities and new subdomains available to their followers.

GOOD DEITIES

See the table on the inside front cover for more information about the following deities.

Apsu: Non-dragon adherents of Apsu are usually humans obsessed with dragonkind. They live to serve or emulate metallic dragons, protecting the lands and people under their care.

Cayden Cailean: Followers of the Drunken Hero strive to protect the right to enjoy life. They defend the weak, destroy threats to freedom, and fight obstacles to having a good time.

Desna: The free spirits who worship the goddess also known as the Song of the Spheres live to discover new and exciting experiences. Along the way they teach others how to find joy in all things and alleviate unhappiness from their lives.

Erastil: The straightforward worshipers of Old Deadeye preserve traditional values, defend rural communities, and teach folk how to provide for themselves and their families.

Iomedae: The righteous who cleave to the Inheritor's dogma eradicate evil and injustice wherever they are found. Her followers do everything in their power to protect the weak while teaching them how to defend themselves.

Kofusachi: Followers of the Laughing God seek to spread happiness and prosperity. They provide blessings for births, weddings, business deals, and journeys and teach that love should not be limited to one partner, or to partners of just one race or gender.

Kurgess: Faithful worshipers of the Strong Man follow the rules of good sportsmanship. They believe in giving everyone a fighting chance and teach others to be gracious losers as well as humble winners.

Milani: The often hidden followers of the Everbloom are rebels and revolutionaries. They oppose despots, organize uprisings, and work in secret to remove the iron gauntlet of tyranny from the world.

Qi Zhong: The Master of Medicine teaches his worshipers to spread knowledge and learning, particularly in the fields of magic and medicine. Though they may take up positions in academic institutions, more often they choose to travel and fill the world with wisdom.

Sarenrae: Worshipers of the Dawnflower are never without hope. They steer others to do good, and strive to better themselves with every dawn.

Shelyn: The artists and lovers who favor the Eternal Rose work to replace ugliness with beauty and despair with hope. They teach others to find beauty in unlikely places, preserve works of art, and ensure lovers have the freedom to express their mutual joy.

Shizuru: Worshipers of the Empress of Heaven live virtuous lives and hope to inspire others to do the same. They teach respect for one's ancestors and the lessons of honorable swordsmanship while always hoping against the need to ever raise a sword in battle.

Torag: The Father of Creation's adherents believe that every moment should have a purpose, whether safeguarding their homes, conquering their enemies, or crafting new tools for the benefit of their communities.

Tsukiyo: The followers of the Prince of the Moon act as intermediaries between the living and the spirit world. They preserve cemeteries, help protect communities from evil spirits, and teach innocents not to be afraid of the dark.

SUBDOMAINS

Presented here are new subdomains that, at your GM's discretion, may be substituted for one of a deity's domains. Suggested deities that may optionally grant the use of the following subdomains are listed in the entry for each subdomain.

COOPERATION SUBDOMAIN

Associated Domain: Community

Associated Deities: Erastil, Kurgess

Replacement Power: The following granted power replaces the calming touch ability of the Community domain.

Synergistic Touch (Sp): You can touch a creature as a standard action to confer upon it the benefits of any one Teamwork feat that you possess. This effect persists for a number of rounds equal to 1/2 your cleric level (minimum 1). You can use this ability a number of times per day equal to 3 + your Wisdom modifier.

Replacement Domain Spells: 1st—*borrow skill*[APG], 2nd—*share language*[APG], 3rd—*coordinated effort*[APG]

DRAGON SUBDOMAIN

Associated Domain: Scalykind

Associated Deities: Apsu

Replacement Power: The following granted power replaces the serpent companion ability of the Scalykind domain.

Dragonbreath (Su): At 4th level, you may use a breath weapon once per day as a standard action. When you gain this ability, choose acid, cold, fire, or electricity—this determines what kind of damage your breath weapon deals. Once you make this choice, you cannot change it later. Your breath weapon fills a 15-foot cone, and deals 3d6 points of damage—this damage increases by 1d6 points at every even-numbered level you gain beyond 4th level. A creature hit by your dragonbreath attack can attempt a Reflex save (DC 10 + 1/2 your cleric level + your Constitution modifier) to take half damage. At 9th level, you can use this ability two times per day, and at 14th level you can use it three times per day.

Replacement Domain Spells: 3rd—*draconic reservoir*APG, 4th—*dragon's breath*APG, 6th—*form of the dragon I*

IMAGINATION SUBDOMAIN

Associated Domain: Luck

Associated Deities: Desna, Kofusachi, Shelyn

Replacement Power: The following granted power replaces the good fortune ability of the Luck domain.

Haze of Daydreams (Su): At 6th level, you can emit a 15-foot-radius haze of daydreams for a number of rounds per day equal to your cleric level. These rounds do not need to be consecutive. Creatures within the haze gain the fascinated condition unless they succeed at a Will save (DC equal to 10 + 1/2 your cleric level + your Wisdom modifier). You may designate a number of creatures equal to your cleric level that are not affected by the haze. The fascinated condition ends immediately when the creatures leave the area or the aura expires.

Replacement Domain Spells: 1st—*silent image*, 2nd—*minor image*, 3rd—*major image*, 5th—*dream*

JUDGMENT SUBDOMAIN

Associated Domain: Law

Associated Deities: Apsu, Iomedae, Torag

Replacement Power: The following granted power replaces the touch of law ability of the Law domain.

Chastisement (Su): As a standard action, you can cast a strengthened spell against a creature that damaged you during the previous round. Such a spell is cast at +1 caster level. This spell must specifically target the creature that damaged you. Area of effect spells cannot be used in conjunction with this ability. You can use this ability a number of times per day equal to 3 + your Wisdom modifier.

Replacement Domain Spells: 2nd—*castigate*APG, 4th—*rebuke*APG, 5th—*mark of justice*

REDEMPTION SUBDOMAIN

Associated Domain: Good

Associated Deities: Iomedae, Sarenrae

Replacement Power: The following granted power replaces the holy lance ability of the Good domain.

Aura of Sanctification (Su): At 8th level, as an immediate action, you can emit a 30-foot-radius aura of sanctification for a number of rounds per day equal to your cleric level. These rounds do not need to be consecutive. Within this aura, effects that are specifically harmful to good-aligned creatures are inverted so that they no longer harm good creatures and instead harm evil creatures. Similarly, effects that are specifically beneficial to evil creatures instead become beneficial only to good creatures.

Replacement Domain Spells: 2nd—*qualm*UC, 4th—*forced repentance*APG, 5th—*atonement*

REVELATION SUBDOMAIN

Associated Domain: Sun

Associated Deities: Iomedae, Sarenrae, Shizuru

Replacement Power: The following granted power replaces the sun's blessing ability of the Sun domain.

Guided Eyes (Su): Perception is always a class skill for you. In addition, whenever you make a skill check to see through a disguise or find something that is hidden or concealed, you gain a +4 sacred bonus on the check.

Replacement Domain Spells: 1st—*detect secret doors*, 2nd—*see invisibility*, 3rd—*banish seeming*APG, 5th—*true seeing*

REVELRY SUBDOMAIN

Associated Domain: Chaos

Associated Deities: Cayden Cailean, Desna, Kofusachi

Replacement Power: The following granted power replaces the chaos blade ability of the Chaos domain.

Intense Celebration (Su): At 8th level, any spells you cast that confer a morale effect upon you or your allies are automatically affected as if by the Extend Spell metamagic feat with no increase in spell level.

Replacement Domain Spells: 2nd—*hideous laughter*, 3rd—*good hope*, 6th—*heroes' feast*, 8th—*irresistible dance*

Fighting the Good Fight

To promote good it is necessary to crush evil, sometimes by coming to the defense of threatened innocents and sometimes more actively. Those who dedicate their lives to these goals sacrifice personal safety and peace in the name of good.

CELESTIAL RAGE POWERS

While others rage in brutality or for the sheer love of violence, good barbarians' fury is fuelled by a sense of justice and righteousness for which they live and die.

Celestial Totem (Su): While raging, the barbarian shines with a righteous light. This effect bestows upon the barbarian a halo of gleaming light that shines as if it were *daylight* and triggers an *invisibility purge* effect in the barbarian's square and each adjacent square. The *invisibility purge* only affects nongood creatures. A barbarian must be at least 8th level to select this rage power.

Celestial Totem, Greater (Su): While raging, the barbarian gains spell resistance equal to 11 + the barbarian's class level against spells with the evil descriptor. She also gains a +2 bonus on all saving throws against spells and effects from evil creatures. A barbarian must have the celestial totem rage power and be at least 12th level to select this rage power.

Celestial Totem, Lesser (Su): While raging, the barbarian benefits from increased magical healing. Whenever she is subject to a spell that cures hit point damage, she heals 1 additional point of damage per caster level. In the case of non-spell healing effects (such as channeled energy or lay on hands), she heals a number of additional points equal to the class level of the character performing the magical healing. This does not affect fast healing or regeneration.

INQUISITIONS

An inquisitor's work may seem unconventional to others, but sometimes to do real, lasting good, it is necessary to engage in actions that appear to cross lines—special tasks require special skills. Living on the sharper, rustier side of purity, inquisitors carry a heavy but still holy burden.

FINAL REST

Deities: Iomedae, Pharasma, Sarenrae

Granted Powers: The dead have paid their dues; there is no need, and no excuse, for them to walk. You protect their rest personally.

Disrupt Animation (Sp): You can use *disrupt undead* as a spell-like ability, adding your wisdom modifier to the damage. You can use this ability a number of times per day equal to 3 + your Wisdom modifier.

Unravel Animation (Su): At 8th level, when you activate your bane ability with undead as the creature type, you can choose for your weapon to instead gain the *disruption* weapon special ability. The DC to resist this effect is equal to 10 + 1/2 your inquisitor level + your Wisdom modifier.

RECOVERY

Deities: Abadar, Erastil, Nivi Rhombodazzle, Shelyn

Granted Powers: Some hunt down secrets, but you focus on the search for more tangible items.

Focused Search (Ex): Once per day, you may designate a person or object as your focus. This takes 1 minute of concentration, during which time you must either picture this item or person if familiar to you, or meditate on the item's or person's description if not. Until you choose a new focus, you gain a bonus equal to half your inquisitor level on Perception checks to see or hear your focus, or when

TAKE THEM ALIVE!

Sometimes capturing an opponent alive protects the greater good, whether by unraveling a larger scheme or showing justice being done.

SUBDUING AN OPPONENT

A creature falls unconscious when it takes a cumulative amount of nonlethal damage that exceeds its current hit points. Any nonlethal damage beyond this becomes lethal damage, making heavy-handed sappings dangerous. Consider these options to incapacitate foes. When using a weapon that normally deals lethal damage, a creature can take a –4 penalty on attack rolls to instead deal nonlethal damage.

Weapons: Bolas (exotic; 1d4 bludgeoning; nonlethal, trip), sap (martial; 1d6 bludgeoning; nonlethal), whip (exotic; 1d4 slashing; disarm, nonlethal, reach, trip)

Feats That Help: Bludgeoner^UC, Golden Legion's Stayed Blade (see below), Improved Unarmed Strike, Knockout Artist^UC, Pinning Knockout^UC, Sap Adept^UC, Sap Master^UC, Stage Combatant^UC

BINDINGS

Various materials and items can be used to restrain creatures.

Manacles: A creature can slip out of manacles with a successful DC 30 Escape Artist check (DC 35 for masterwork manacles), and they require a successful DC 26 Strength check to burst (DC 28 for masterwork manacles). Mithral manacles are a bit stronger and can be burst with a successful DC 30 Strength check. Manacles for large creatures cost 10 times the listed price.

Ropes and Chains: Ropes have an escape DC of 20 + the binder's CMB. Hemp rope will hold most humans and can be burst with a successful DC 23 Strength check. Silk rope can be burst with a successful DC 24 Strength check. Spider's silk rope can be burst with a successful DC 25 Strength check. A bit stronger than the strongest rope, chain offers a break DC of 26.

---

using Survival to track your focus or a creature with your focus in its possession. This bonus stacks with that gained from the track special ability.

Locate Focus (Sp): At 8th level, once per day you may use either *locate creature* or *locate object* as a spell-like ability using your current focus as the target. The range of this effect is 1 mile per level.

FEATS

The following feats help good characters in their fight.

GOLDEN LEGION'S STAYED BLADE

When you're dealing with large and secretive organizations, a dead enemy is just a corpse, but a captured enemy can be a tool.

Prerequisite: Base attack bonus +3.

Benefit: If you deal an amount of damage to a creature that would slay it outright, you can pull that attack, instead dealing only enough damage to reduce its hit points to –1, and leave it stable.

LASTWALL PHALANX (TEAMWORK)

When battling the terrifying hordes of Belkzen, you find strength in your shield brothers and sisters.

Prerequisites: Base attack bonus +3, good alignment.

Benefit: You gain a sacred bonus to your AC against the attacks of evil creatures and a sacred bonus to saves against the spells and abilities of evil creatures equal to the number of adjacent allies who also have this feat.

LEGACY OF OZEM

Your purity is so great that the blades and bows of long-forgotten heroes sing to you as if they had been made for your righteous hands.

Prerequisites: Base attack bonus +5, good alignment.

Benefit: When using good-aligned weapons, including those under the effects of a *bless weapon* spell, you gain a +1 sacred bonus on damage rolls.

PEACEMAKER

Your words of peace ring true and are much more difficult for others to resist.

Prerequisites: Charisma 13, good alignment.

Benefit: The DC to resist spells you cast to ensure peace or force aggressive creatures to become peaceful increases by +2. This affects spells that dissuade creatures from aggressive actions without exerting long-term or absolute control over them, and without leaving them defenseless. These spells include, but are not limited to, *calm animals*, *calm emotions*, *command*, *compassionate ally*^UM, *enthrall*, *euphoric tranquility*^UM, *sanctuary*, and *serenity*^UM.

SIPHON POISON

You can remove poison from afflicted creatures.

Benefit: As a full-round action, you can remove an injury poison from a helpless or willing creature's bloodstream with a successful Heal check. The DC of this check is equal to the poison's DC. You can only draw out poison in this way within the first 2 rounds of when the target was poisoned. If the check is successful, the creature no longer suffers any additional effects from the poison. By performing this action, you do not risk poisoning yourself.

WORLDWOUND WALKER

Your purity always remains a blessing, even when you're surrounded by creatures that despise it.

Prerequisites: 5 or more Hit Dice, good alignment.

Benefit: You can alter the essence of your being to lessen the effects of spells designed to harm good creatures. When affected by spells and effects that behave differently according to alignment (such as *unholy word* or *protection from good*), you can choose whether you are considered good or neutral. This ability does not actually change your alignment or fool divinations, nor does it permit you to overcome alignment requirements for the use of magic items, class abilities, and so on.

Glory and beatification are for paladins and martyrs—not every hero desires recognition. Many acts of great good go unnoticed, and for pure-hearted scoundrels, operating in shadow and silence, this is exactly how they like it.

ALCHEMICAL DISCOVERIES

Alchemists with a good alignment have shared the following alchemical discoveries with their brethren. Discoveries marked with an asterisk (*) do not stack. Only one such discovery can be applied to an individual bomb. The DC of any saving throw called for by a discovery is equal to 10 + 1/2 the alchemist's level + the alchemist's Intelligence modifier.

Celestial Poisons (Su): The alchemist is able to infuse poisons with celestial power so they can affect evil creatures that are normally immune to poison. Any poison the alchemist administers to a weapon can affect undead and evil outsiders, bypassing their inherent immunities. Magical effects that negate poisons still apply. If a creature fails its save, the poison acts as normal, but may have no effect on the creature, depending on the effect of the poison (such as dealing Constitution damage to undead). An alchemist must be at least 8th level before selecting this discovery.

Change Alignment (Su): Once per day as part of his preparation of infusions, the alchemist can brew an infusion that shifts the imbiber's alignment to good. This change in alignment lasts for 10 minutes per alchemist level. An unwilling creature receives a Will save to resist this change. The alchemist may have only one such infusion at any one time. The effects of this infusion may have serious repercussions for a creature suddenly struggling with a new outlook. Many see it as little more than forced insanity, and some good faiths outlaw its use. An alchemist must be at least 12th level and have the infusion discovery before selecting this discovery.

Holy Bombs*: When the alchemist creates a bomb, he can choose to have it deal good divine damage. Evil creatures that take a direct hit from a holy bomb must succeed at a Fortitude save or be staggered on their next turn. Against neutral creatures, holy bombs deal half damage, and such targets are not affected by their staggering effect. Holy bombs have no effect on good-aligned creatures. An alchemist must be at least 8th level before selecting this discovery.

Ranged Baptism (Su): When the alchemist uses holy water as a splash weapon, any squares subject to its effects (including creatures affected by splash damage) or that contain creatures subject to its effects are also affected as if by *consecrate*, for a number of rounds equal to the alchemist's Intelligence modifier. Undead struck by holy water remain affected by the *consecrate* effect even if they leave the affected area. An alchemist must be at least 4th level before selecting this discovery.

GRAND DISCOVERY

The following discovery is available to alchemists who reach 20th level.

Change Alignment, Greater (Su): The effects of the alchemist's change alignment infusion become permanent and can only be reversed by a *wish* or *miracle*. A permanent, forced change of alignment may be devastating, and some believe it is little better than zealous slavery or mind control. Others consider a good alignment brought about by any means but purity of heart an affront to freedom. This discovery remains controversial at best. An alchemist must take the change alignment discovery and the infusion discovery before selecting this discovery.

MASTERPIECES

The songs of the Inner Sea are rich with tales of conflicts between good and evil. Some of these songs have become little more than simple children's rhymes, but others, at the hands of pure-hearted musicians, have become hymns of peace and purity for those who strive to bring good to all of Golarion.

Clamor of the Heavens (Percussion, Sing)

This confusing dirge of melody and counter-melody was composed for choirs celebrating the various martyrs of Ragathiel. It is intended to praise and magnify the glory of the empyreal lord, but to the uninitiated it sounds like a battle hymn. In fact, in Varisia, this is what the song has become to many.

Prerequisites: Perform (percussion or sing) 10 ranks.

Cost: 5th-level bard spell known.

Effect: Evil creatures that hear the performance and fail a Will save against the effect are blinded and deafened for the duration. On a successful save, they are shaken instead. Undead or creatures with the evil subtype that fail their saves are stunned for the duration, while those that succeed are staggered.

Use: 3 bardic performance rounds, +1 round per additional round of duration.

Action: 3 full rounds.

Life Budding in Salted Earth (Sing, String, Wind)

This delicate tune suggests the determined sprouting of seedlings through barren, rocky soil. Both its motif and effects are popular in Rahadoum, where the tune is also known as "Spring Inside."

Prerequisites: Perform (sing), Perform (string), or Perform (wind) 4 ranks.

Cost: Feat or 3rd-level bard spell known.

Effect: This masterpiece grants all allies within 30 feet fast healing 1 for as long as the bard maintains the performance. He may increase the cost per round of the performance up to a total number equal to half his bard level to increase the fast healing by 1 for each additional round expended.

Use: 1 bardic performance round per round, plus 1 or more additional uses per round to increase the duration of this effect.

Action: 1 standard action.

ROGUE TALENTS

The following rogue talents complement good rogues. Talents marked with an asterisk (*) add effects to a rogue's sneak attack. Only one of these talents can be applied to an individual attack, and the decision must be made before the attack roll is made.

Sacred Sneak Attack (Su): When making a sneak attack against an undead creature or evil outsider, the rogue's sneak attack damage is considered good-aligned for the purpose of overcoming damage reduction. Normal weapon damage is unaffected for this attack. A rogue must have a good alignment to select this rogue talent.

Sacrifice Self (Ex): A rogue who makes a successful Reflex save against an area effect can ignore the benefits of her evasion ability to shield an adjacent ally against the effect, essentially halving the damage that ally would normally take. A rogue with improved evasion can attempt a secondary save against her ally's damage. If the save is successful, neither she nor her ally takes any damage. A rogue must have evasion in order to select this talent, and she must have improved evasion to benefit from the secondary effect.

Stem the Flow (Su): When making a successful sneak attack against a creature with the ability to channel energy, the rogue may forgo 3d6 points of sneak attack damage to instead prevent the target from channeling energy for a number of rounds equal to half her rogue level.

Sublime Spellcraft

Magic is neither good nor evil, and while the great effort sometimes required to master arcane ability often concentrates it into the hands of only the very determined, it is just as likely that such determination will be turned to good as to evil.

SUMMONER EVOLUTIONS

The following new evolutions can be taken by any eidolon that meets the prerequisites.

2-Point Evolution

The following evolution costs 2 points from the eidolon's evolution pool.

Alignment Smite (Su): Choose a single alignment component that opposes one of the summoner's own.

Once per day as a swift action, the eidolon chooses one target within sight. If this target's alignment matches that chosen for this ability, the eidolon deals an additional +1d6 points of damage with one of its natural weapons. This attack is treated as good-aligned for the purposes of overcoming damage reduction. The alignment smite persists until the target is dead or the eidolon is dismissed. At 10th level, the summoner may spend 1 additional evolution point to allow the eidolon a second daily use of this ability. The summoner must be at least 5th level before selecting this evolution. Evil or true neutral summoners cannot select this evolution.

3-Point Evolutions

The following evolutions cost 3 points from the eidolon's evolution pool.

Sacrifice (Su): An eidolon can sacrifice its own hit points to heal another creature. As a standard action, the eidolon can sacrifice up to 2 hit points per Hit Die and then touch the target creature, thereby healing the creature for half the amount sacrificed.

Celestial Appearance (Ex): The eidolon appears as a celestial creature and manifests some of the abilities of a celestial. Spells and effects that target creatures with the good subtype or have specific effects against such creatures affect the eidolon as if it were a celestial. The eidolon gains a +2 bonus on saves against disease, petrification, poison, and electricity spells and effects. It also gains spell resistance equal to 5 + its HD against spells with the evil descriptor.

At 7th level, by spending 2 additional evolution points, this bonus on saves is increased to +4 and the spell resistance is extended to affect any spells and effects from evil creatures.

At 12th level, by spending 2 additional evolution points, this protection is increased to immunity against these attacks and the spell resistance is increased to 11 + its HD (the summoner must pay for the 7th-level upgrade before paying for this 12th-level upgrade). The summoner must be good-aligned to select this evolution.

WITCH PATRONS AND HEXES

A witch's powers are strange and mysterious to non-witches, and their source is sometimes an enigma even to herself. Patrons are rarely deities on Golarion, but occasionally their servants or aspects empower good witches. More often patronage comes from mysterious, enigmatic entities representing powerful ideals.

Witch Patron Themes

The following are alternative patron themes that a good witch can choose.

Boundaries: 2nd—*protection from evil*, 4th—*see invisibility*, 6th—*magic circle against evil*, 8th—*dimensional anchor*, 10th—*control summoned creature*^{UM}, 12th—*banishment*, 14th—*ethereal jaunt*, 16th—*dimensional lock*, 18th—*gate*.

Devotion: 2nd—*divine favor*, 4th—*martyr's bargain*^{ISM}, 6th—*magic vestment*, 8th—*greater magic weapon*, 10th—*flame strike*, 12th—*mass bull's strength*, 14th—*bestow grace of the champion*^{UM}, 16th—*holy aura*, 18th—*mass heal*.

Peace: 2nd—*sanctuary*, 4th—*calm emotions*, 6th—*wind wall*, 8th—*dismissal*, 10th—*serenity*^{UM}, 12th—*word of recall*, 14th—*forcecage*, 16th—*euphoric tranquility*^{APG}, 18th—*antipathy*.

Hexes

The following hexes complement witches who have a good alignment. The save to resist a hex is equal to 10 + 1/2 the witch's level + the witch's Intelligence modifier.

Aura of Purity (Su): The witch's aura purifies the air around her. Diseases, inhaled poisons, and noxious gaseous effects (such as *stinking cloud*) are negated in a 10-foot aura around the witch for a number of minutes equal to her level. This duration does not need to be consecutive, but it must be spent in 1-minute increments. Effects caused by spells whose level is more than half the witch's class level are unaffected.

Peacebond (Su): A witch can use this hex on a creature to prevent it from drawing a weapon for a number of rounds equal to the witch's level. This hex has no effect on natural weapons or weapons already in a creature's hands, but does prevent an archer from drawing arrows. A Will save negates this effect, and whether or not the save is successful, a creature cannot be the target of this hex again for 1 day.

Major Hexes

Starting at 10th level, and every 2 levels thereafter, a witch can choose one of the following major hexes whenever she could select a new hex.

Witch's Bounty (Su): The witch may bless a bush, plant, or tree that is planted in the ground, so that it creates a plentiful harvest. Each day at dawn, this blessed bush grows a number of *goodberries* equal to twice her witch level. Berries on the tree remain until they are picked, but the tree can never manifest a number of berries greater than twice her level at one time. The witch may only have one witch's bounty active at a time, but can shift her blessing to a new plant with a ritual requiring 1 hour.

Witch's Charge (Su): Once per day when preparing spells, a witch can designate a willing creature as her charge. She gains a constant *status* effect on this creature and can target it with beneficial touch spells from a range of 30 feet. The creature remains her charge until she designates a new one.

Grand Hexes

Starting at 18th level, a witch can choose one of the following grand hexes whenever she could select a new hex.

Curse of Nonviolence (Su): The witch can curse a creature to prevent it from attacking innocents. If the target fails its Will save, it cannot take violent actions or do anything destructive against any creature with fewer Hit Dice than itself. If another creature takes hostile action against the cursed creature, the cursed creature can act normally in regard to that creature only. This is an abjuration effect. The curse is permanent but can be removed with a *break enchantment*, *miracle*, or *wish* spell. Whether or not the save is successful, a creature cannot be the target of this hex again for 1 day.

Lay to Rest (Sp): The witch may target a single undead creature with this hex as if with an *undeath to death* spell. A Will save negates this effect. Whether or not the save is successful, a creature cannot be the target of this hex again for 1 day.

WIZARD ARCANE DISCOVERIES

Arcane discoveries are the results of wizards' obsessive research into magic. A wizard can learn one of the following arcane discoveries in place of a regular feat or wizard bonus feat. More information about arcane discoveries can be found on page 86 of *Pathfinder RPG Ultimate Magic*.

Steward of the Great Beyond: Whenever a creature attempts to use a teleportation effect or summon a creature within 30 feet of you, you may attempt to block the effect. Make an opposed caster level check (1d20 + caster level) as an immediate action. If the check succeeds, the spell or effect fails and is wasted; otherwise, it is unaffected. You can use this ability once per day plus one additional time for every 5 wizard levels you possess beyond 10th. You must be at least a 9th-level wizard to select this discovery.

Yuelral's Blessing: You cast any spells that appear on both the wizard and druid spell lists at +1 caster level and with +1 to the save DC. In addition, you may replace the material component of any arcane spell with gems of the same value. You must be at least a 5th-level wizard to select this discovery.

Spells of the Just

Good-aligned spellcasters across Golarion—and beyond—research spells to help their fight against evil. Some allow you to take on the characteristics of celestials, while others promote peace and mercy. All of the following spells have the good descriptor.

ACCEPT AFFLICTION

School conjuration (healing) [good]; **Level** bard 3, cleric 3, druid 3, paladin 3, witch 3

Casting Time 1 standard action

Components V, S, M/DF (dove's heart)

Range touch

Target creature touched

Duration instantaneous

Saving Throw Fortitude negates (harmless); **Spell Resistance** yes (harmless)

The caster can transfer the effects of afflictions such as curses, diseases, and poisons from the target creature to himself. This spell can also transfer the blinded, deafened, fatigued, nauseated, shaken, and sickened conditions. All aspects of the transferred afflictions (save DCs, remaining duration, removal conditions, and so on) remain the same, but affect the caster instead of the original target. After transferring the affliction or condition, the caster is free to cure it in any way he can.

ANGELIC ASPECT

School transmutation [good]; **Level** cleric 5, paladin 3, sorcerer/wizard 5

This spell functions like *lesser angelic aspect*, except you gain low-light vision, darkvision 60, resistance to acid 10, resistance to cold 10, and DR 5/evil, and you sprout white feathered wings allowing you to fly at a speed of 30 feet with average maneuverability. In addition, your natural weapons and any weapons you wield are considered good-aligned for the purpose of overcoming damage reduction.

ANGELIC ASPECT, GREATER

School transmutation [good]; **Level** cleric 8, paladin 4, sorcerer/wizard 8

This spell functions like *lesser angelic aspect*, except you gain low-light vision; darkvision 60 feet; DR 10/evil; immunity to acid, cold, and petrification; resistance to electricity 10 and fire 10; a +4 racial bonus on saves against poison; and protective aura and truespeech as supernatural abilities for the duration of the spell. Also, your wings give you a fly speed of 60 feet with good maneuverability.

Protective aura provides a +4 deflection bonus to AC and a +4 resistance bonus on saving throws against attacks made or effects created by evil creatures to anyone within 20 feet. Otherwise, it functions as a *magic circle against evil* and a *lesser globe of invulnerability*, both with a radius of 20 feet.

Truespeech allows you to speak with any creature that has a language, as though using the *tongues* spell.

ANGELIC ASPECT, LESSER

School transmutation [good]; **Level** cleric 2, paladin 2, sorcerer/wizard 2

Casting Time 1 standard action

Components V, S

Range personal

Target you

Duration 1 minute/level (D)

Saving Throw none; **Spell Resistance** no

You take on an aspect of an angelic being, including some of its physical characteristics. You gain low-light vision, resistance to acid 5, resistance to cold 5, and the benefits of *protection from evil*.

ARCHON'S TRUMPET

School evocation [good, sonic]; **Level** bard 5, cleric 7, paladin 4, sorcerer/wizard 7

Casting Time 1 standard action

Components V, S

Range 30 ft.
Area cone-shaped burst
Duration instantaneous
Saving Throw Fortitude negates; **Spell Resistance** yes

Upon hearing a booming report, as if from a trumpet archon's mighty horn, all creatures in the area of the burst are paralyzed for 1d4 rounds.

BURST OF RADIANCE

School evocation [good, light]; **Level** cleric 2, druid 2, sorcerer/wizard 2
Casting Time 1 standard action
Components V, S, M/DF (a piece of flint and a pinch of silver dust)
Range long (400 ft. + 40 ft./level)
Area 10-ft.-radius burst
Duration instantaneous
Saving Throw Reflex partial; **Spell Resistance** yes

This spell fills the area with a brilliant flash of shimmering light. Creatures in the area are blinded for 1d4 rounds, or dazzled for 1d4 rounds if they succeed at a Reflex save. Evil creatures in the area of the burst take 1d4 points of damage per caster level (max 5d4), whether they succeed at the Reflex save or not.

CHAINS OF LIGHT

School conjuration (creation) [good]; **Level** cleric 6, inquisitor 5, paladin 4, sorcerer/wizard 6
Casting Time 1 standard action
Components V, S, F (a length of fine golden chain)
Range short (25 ft. + 5 ft./level)
Target one creature
Duration 1 round/level (D)
Saving Throw Reflex negates; **Spell Resistance** no

A creature targeted by this spell is held immobile by glowing golden chains composed of pure light. The creature is paralyzed and held in place, but may attempt a new saving throw each round to end the effect. While held by the golden chains, a creature cannot use any sort of extradimensional travel, such as *astral projection, blink, dimension door, ethereal jaunt, etherealness, gate, maze, plane shift, shadow walk, teleport,* and similar spells and spell-like abilities. The spell does not affect creatures that are already in ethereal or astral form when the spell is cast.

HYMN OF MERCY

School enchantment (compulsion) [good, mind-affecting]; **Level** bard 5, cleric 5
Casting Time 1 standard action
Components V, S
Range 30 ft.
Area 30-ft.-radius burst centered on you
Duration 1 round/level (D)
Saving Throw Will negates; **Spell Resistance** yes

This spell functions like *touch of mercy*, except as noted above.

HYMN OF PEACE

School abjuration [good]; **Level** bard 6, cleric 7
Casting Time 1 standard action
Components V, S

UTUNZAJI HEKIMA: THE PRESERVATION OF WISDOM

The ancient Mwangi wizard Old-Mage Jatembe is said to have salvaged much of the culture of the first Mwangi civilization and prevented humanity from backsliding into barbarism after that empire was obliterated by Earthfall, the event that created the Inner Sea. He is also credited with penning an invaluable collection of scrolls known as the Utunzaji Hekima. According to legend, these 111 scrolls contained the most complete record of the mage's insights ever put to paper, including everything from transcripts of conversations with angels and lesser deities to unique research into the nature of magic and its place in the world. Sadly, most of the scrolls have been lost or destroyed over the millennia, but the few that are preserved at Magaambya—the arcane academy Old-Mage Jatembe established—or scattered across Golarion contain lore undreamed of by modern scholars.

The Utunzaji Hekima scroll known as Usafi was recently recovered from one of the demon-haunted ruins littering the trackless Mwangi Jungle. It contains the spells found in this section along with notes on their most efficient application and an inspired treatise on the moral implications and responsibilities facing a principled spellcaster. A spellcaster who studies the scroll for at least 1 hour (this can be while preparing or praying for spells) casts spells with the good descriptor at +1 caster level but casts spells with the evil descriptor at −2 caster levels for 24 hours or until she prepares spells again.

Range 40 ft.
Area 40-ft.-radius burst centered on you
Duration 1 round/level (D)
Saving Throw Will negates; **Spell Resistance** yes

Each time a subject of this spell attempts to attack another creature or object, or otherwise perform an aggressive or damaging action toward a creature or object, it must attempt a Will save. If the save succeeds, the subject can attack normally. If the save fails, the subject cannot follow through with the attack and loses that part of its action. Creatures not taking violent actions are unaffected by this spell.

TOUCH OF MERCY

School enchantment (compulsion) [good, mind-affecting]; **Level** bard 2, cleric 2, sorcerer/wizard 2
Casting Time 1 standard action
Components V, S, DF
Range touch
Target one creature
Duration 1 round/level (D)
Saving Throw Will negates; **Spell Resistance** yes

The target creature deals only nonlethal damage with all of its weapon attacks. Damage taken by creatures or objects that are not subject to nonlethal damage is not converted to nonlethal and remains lethal damage. The weapon retains all of its other normal properties.

Tools for Good

While strength of will, a passion for righteousness, and dedication to peace fuel good-aligned characters in their fight against evil, they must also rely on physical tools. The following weapon special abilities and magic items help adventurers fight the good fight.

WEAPON SPECIAL ABILITIES

These new weapon special abilities follow all of the rules for weapon special abilities found on page 134 of *Pathfinder RPG Ultimate Equipment*.

COMPASSIONATE		PRICE +1 bonus
AURA moderate conjuration	CL 7th	WEIGHT —

A *compassionate* weapon has the power to save a foe from the brink of death. When a successful hit from a compassionate weapon would bring a creature to –1 or fewer hit points, that creature is automatically stabilized. This ability can be suppressed at will as a free action.

CONSTRUCTION REQUIREMENTS	COST +1 bonus

Craft Magic Arms and Armor, *stabilize*

REDEEMED		PRICE +3 bonus
AURA strong abjuration and evocation [good]	CL 12th	WEIGHT —

A *redeemed* weapon was once a corrupt *unholy* weapon. The taint of evil has been purged from it, however, and the weapon is now in all ways a *holy* weapon, dealing an additional 2d6 points of damage against all creatures of evil alignment. In addition, the wielder gains a sacred bonus on saving throws equal to the weapon's enhancement bonus against the spells and abilities of evil outsiders and a +5 competence bonus on Knowledge (planes) checks to identify evil outsiders and their special powers or vulnerabilities. When the *redeemed* weapon special ability is added to an *unholy* weapon, the weapon loses the *unholy* property and gains the *redeemed* property, and the crafter must pay the price of adding a +1 enhancement bonus to the weapon.

CONSTRUCTION REQUIREMENTS	COST +3 bonus

Craft Magic Arms and Armor, *consecrate*, *holy smite*, creator must be good

MAGIC ITEMS

The following new wondrous items complement good-aligned characters.

BONDBREAKER'S BOOTS		PRICE 1,600 GP
SLOT feet	CL 1st	WEIGHT 1 lb.
AURA faint transmutation		

These leather boots bear a knife motif worked into their durable blue leather. Three times per day, the wearer can speak a command word as a swift action, causing a serrated knife to fly from the boots and instantly slice through any nonmagical bond currently restraining the wearer. The knife conjured from *bondbreaker's boots* can cut through brambles, ropes, tanglefoot bags, vines, webs, or any other similar nonmagical item restraining the wearer, but cannot help when the owner is actively restrained by a creature. *Bondbreaker's boots* also cannot free the wearer if manacles or chains restrain her.

CONSTRUCTION REQUIREMENTS	COST 800 GP

Craft Wondrous Item, *unseen servant*

DEVIL'S KEY		PRICE 66,750 GP
SLOT none	CL 17th	WEIGHT 5 lbs.
AURA strong abjuration, conjuration, and evocation		

Forged with a wicked barbed end that resembles a key, this +2 *redeemed longsword* was once the unholy sword of a diabolist—before a party of adventurers retrieved it from his corpse and repurposed the weapon for good. The *devil's key* is designed to permanently slay evil outsiders by bringing the fight to their plane of origin so they can be killed outright.

Once per day as a swift action after a successful attack against an evil outsider, the wielder can activate the sword to plane shift the wielder and the target of the attack to the creature's home plane. The targeted outsider can resist this effect with a successful DC 20 Will save. Once the target of this ability is slain by the wielder, the sword activates another *plane shift* as an immediate action that brings the wielder back to the exact spot it previously left.

CONSTRUCTION REQUIREMENTS	COST 33,533 GP

Craft Magic Arms and Armor, *consecrate*, *holy smite*, *plane shift*, creator must be good

EQUALIZER SHIELD		PRICE 120,830 GP
SLOT shield	CL 12th	WEIGHT 23 lbs.
AURA strong abjuration		

Shined to a mirror finish and fitted with supple leather straps, this +1 *mithral tower shield* displays no decoration or markings on its highly reflective surface. Once per day, the bearer of this shield can issue a challenge to a foe and ring the shield like a gong, resulting in a resonating blast that negates all magic in a 10-foot radius, as per *antimagic field*. This effect lasts for 1 minute.

CONSTRUCTION REQUIREMENTS	COST 60,930 GP

Craft Magic Arms and Armor, *antimagic field*

FIELD MEDIC'S BREASTPLATE

	PRICE 52,900 GP
SLOT armor	**CL** 7th	**WEIGHT** 30 lbs.
AURA moderate abjuration, faint conjuration		

This battered yet lovingly polished *+1 breastplate* is marked by three chipped glass circles set over the heart, each of a different color. Three times per day, the wearer may tap a circle to activate it, enveloping her in a shimmering aura that protects her from harm. The wearer gains DR 10/— and is protected if she were under the effects of a *globe of invulnerability* spell. The effect ends as soon as the wearer makes an offensive action or casts an offensive spell, or after 1 minute. In addition, whenever the wearer casts a cure spell or administers a cure potion while under this effect, she may add one additional die to the total amount of damage healed.

CONSTRUCTION REQUIREMENTS	**COST** 26,450 GP

Craft Magic Arms and Armor, *cure light wounds, sanctuary*

MANTLE OF THE PROTECTOR

	PRICE 12,200 GP
SLOT shoulders	**CL** 7th	**WEIGHT** 10 lbs.
AURA moderate abjuration and conjuration		

This silvery cloak has steel pauldrons built into it, and always seems to fit a little too loosely, no matter who happens to be wearing it. At the start of each day, the owner of a *mantle of the protector* may spend 10 minutes attuning the mantle to his armor and shield. He may then lend his attuned mantle to an ally, who can activate it as an immediate action at any time to gain the owner's armor and shield bonus as well as any other special properties the armor may have for 10 minutes. When the mantle is activated this way, the owner's armor and shield go dormant, and he loses any benefits they may provide for 1 minute.

CONSTRUCTION REQUIREMENTS	**COST** 6,100 GP

Craft Wondrous Item, *shield other*

PHOENIX ARMOR

	PRICE 36,130 GP
SLOT armor	**CL** 9th	**WEIGHT** 50 lbs.
AURA moderate evocation and transmutation		

This brilliant golden *+2 fire resistant full plate* is decorated with an ornate feather motif curling across its surface and seems to radiate warmth. Once per day, the wearer can invoke the name of the phoenix that blessed the armor and bring the might of that phoenix against the wearer's foe. Activating the armor causes it to ignite, wreathing the wearer in red-gold flames as if under the effects of *fire shield*. In addition, great golden wings unfold out of the back of the armor, allowing the wearer to fly as per the spell. Both of these effects last for 9 rounds.

CONSTRUCTION REQUIREMENTS	**COST** 18,890 GP

Craft Magic Arms and Armor, *fire shield, fly*

RYTHIUS, THE KYTON SCOURGE

	PRICE 53,000 GP
SLOT none	**CL** 12th	**WEIGHT** 2 lbs.
AURA strong abjuration and evocation		

Once possessed by a brijidine azata dedicated to ending the depredations of kytons, this potent magic weapon now holds a portion of her essence. This *+1 shock whip* is woven from green leather and crackles with electricity, seemingly writhing of its own volition. Three times per day, when the wielder uses *Rythius* to successfully trip a creature, the target of the trip attack is subject to a *dimensional anchor* effect. The wielder can choose to suppress this ability as a swift action.

Furthermore, in the hands of a wielder with a good alignment, the weapon becomes a *+1 kyton bane shock whip*. *Rythius* is infused with good, and as a result it bestows 1 negative level on any nongood creature wielding it. This negative level persists as long as the weapon is wielded and disappears when the item is put away. The negative level cannot be overcome in any way (including by means of *restoration* spells) while it is wielded.

CONSTRUCTION REQUIREMENTS	**COST** 26,650 GP

Craft Magic Arms and Armor, *dimensional anchor, holy smite*, creator must be good

SERAPHIC PISTOL

	PRICE 37,550 GP
SLOT none	**CL** 6th	**WEIGHT** 5 lbs.
AURA moderate transmutation		

The gold-washed barrel of this elegant *+2 double-barreled pistol* always catches the light, and its maple grip feels pleasantly warm to the touch. When its wielder successfully bypasses an evil creature's damage reduction with a single attack, the creature's skin cracks into fissures of golden light. This light negates the creature's DR for the gunslinger and her allies, fading away after 1 minute.

CONSTRUCTION REQUIREMENTS	**COST** 19,800 GP

Craft Magic Arms and Armor, *versatile weapon*

STAFF OF THE FREED MAN

	PRICE 51,688 GP
SLOT none	**CL** 17th	**WEIGHT** 5 lbs.
AURA moderate varies		

Just over 7 feet tall and topped with what looks like a large iron skeleton key, this unassuming oaken staff appears to be nothing but a common walking stick. It allows use of the following spells:

- *Detect secret doors* (2 charges)
- *Knock* (2 charges)
- *Passwall* (3 charges)
- *Freedom* (5 charges)

CONSTRUCTION REQUIREMENTS	**COST** 25,840 GP

Craft Staff, *detect secret doors, freedom, knock, passwall*

Deceitful, daring, and diminutive, kobolds—those infamous, deep-dwelling inhabitants of the Darklands—creep into your campaign with *Pathfinder Player Companion: Kobolds of Golarion*. Learn the dastardly ways and sinister secrets of the kobolds of the Pathfinder campaign setting, including where they live, how they fight, and what insidious designs they have on the world above. Use these secrets to get the edge on kobold foes, or use new options for playing your own kobold characters to wield them against your own enemies. Goblins aren't the only half-sized horrors on Golarion—unleash the unpredictable cunning of kobolds with *Pathfinder Player Companion: Kobolds of Golarion*!

WOULD YOU LIKE TO KNOW MORE?

Being good isn't always easy, and staying good can prove to be a greater challenge than expected in the dark and ugly world of an adventurer. Someone on the path of good can always look to gods and organizations in the battle to turn back evil's tide.

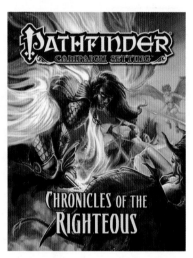

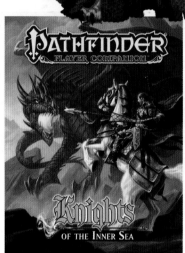

Need a bit more faith in your life? Look no further than *Pathfinder Player Companion: Faiths of Purity*! Learn more about the good-aligned deities on Golarion and how their religions promote goodness.

Goodness is not just the province of mortals. Denizens of the planes have long waged a war against evil, and you can read more about their struggles in *Pathfinder Campaign Setting: Chronicles of the Righteous*.

Golarion is a hotbed of conflict between the forces of good and those who commit evil. Learn more about the various knightly orders that hope to turn the tide in *Pathfinder Player Companion: Knights of the Inner Sea*.